CAL RIPKEN JR.

BASEBALL'S IRON MAN

BY BILL GUTMAN

Millbrook Sports World
The Millbrook Press
Brookfield, Connecticut

Library of Congress Cataloging-in-Publication Data
Gutman, Bill.
Cal Ripken Jr. : baseball's iron man / Bill Gutman.
p. cm. — (Millbrook sports world)
Includes index.
Summary: Covers the life of the Baltimore Orioles star shortstop, from
his childhood in a baseball family to his own successful career, including
his breaking of the record for most consecutive games played.
ISBN 0-7613-0416-9 (lib. bdg.). — ISBN 0-7613-0380-4 (pbk.)
1. Ripken, Cal, 1960-   —Juvenile literature. 2. Baseball players—United
States—Biography—Juvenile literature. 3. Baltimore Orioles (Baseball
team)—History—Juvenile literature. [1. Ripken, Cal, 1960-   .
2. Baseball players.] I. Title. II. Series.
GV865.R47G88 1998   796.357'092—dc21
[B] 98-9857 CIP AC

Cover photographs courtesy of © Reuters/Ray Stubblevine/Archive
Photos; Focus on Sports (inset)

Photographs courtesy of Focus on Sports: p. 3; AP/Wide World
Photos: pp. 4, 15, 22, 27, 34, 37, 39; Seth Poppel Yearbook
Archives: pp. 8, 10; Democrat and Chronicle (Kevin Higley): p. 14;
© Crandall and Associates: pp. 16, 44; UPI/Corbis-Bettmann: p. 19;
© Gregory Heisler/Outline: p. 23; Allsport: pp. 24-25 (© Otto Greule,
Jr.), 30 (© Rick Stewart), 32 (© Doug Pensinger), 46 (© Otto Greule);
Reuters/Joe Giza/Archive Photos: pp. 41, 43

Published by The Millbrook Press, Inc.
2 Old New Milford Road
Brookfield, Connecticut 06804

CAL RIPKEN JR.

One of the great sporting events of the 1990s took place at Camden Yards at Baltimore on September 6, 1995. That was the night Cal Ripken Jr. played in his 2,131st game to become baseball's new "Iron Man." Before the game began, Cal autographed a special baseball for President Bill Clinton, as the president's daughter, Chelsea, and Vice President Al Gore look on.

On September 6, 1995, the Baltimore Orioles were hosting the California Angels at Camden Yards in Baltimore. That season had been a disappointing one for the Orioles. The team was struggling just to finish at .500, winning as many games as they lost, and there was not much hope that they would be part of the playoffs. By all outward appearances, it was a late-season game that didn't mean much to a team with little chance at the postseason.

In the fourth inning, Orioles shortstop Cal Ripken Jr. was at bat, facing the Angels' righthanded pitcher Shawn Boskie. Baltimore had a scant 2–1 lead. Boskie ran the count to three balls and no strikes. Ripken stepped out of the batter's box and looked down at the third-base coach. He wanted to see if he had the hit sign on the upcoming 3–0 pitch. Sure enough, he did.

High up in the Orioles' radio broadcasting booth, a special guest of the team was also commenting on the likelihood of Ripken swinging. "Ripken is always trying to win the game," the guest commentator said. "If [Boskie] throws him a ball, he will take it."

But Boskie thought differently. Figuring Ripken wouldn't be swinging in a close game, Boskie threw a fastball down the middle. The righthanded-batting Ripken sprang to life. He stepped purposefully into the pitch and whipped his bat around. The ball was hit high and deep to left field, and sailed into the stands with room to spare. Cal Ripken began to circle the bases as the full house at Camden Yards erupted in a roar that could be heard for miles.

But why that reaction in an insignificant September game? And why a capacity crowd if the Orioles were out of the playoff picture? The reason was simple: The game was a historic occasion to be treasured forever. That's why the special guest in the broadcast booth was none other than Bill Clinton, president of the United States.

Everyone on hand had come to honor Cal Ripken Jr. It wasn't because he was at the end of his outstanding career. And it wasn't because his home run had any special meaning except helping the Orioles to win the game, 4–2. All of baseball was about to honor Cal Ripken for simply showing up at the ballpark every day and playing. In fact, Ripken had shown up and played every day for more than 13 years. It culminated in that ball game of September 6, 1995, the day that Ripken broke one of baseball's most cherished records.

That game was Cal Ripken Jr.'s 2,131st consecutive baseball game. He had broken the record set by the immortal Lou Gehrig of the New York Yankees nearly a half-century earlier. Because of his durability, Gehrig had been known as the "Iron Horse."

Now, Cal Ripken Jr. was baseball's new Iron Man.

A TRAVELING FAMILY

When Violet Gross married Cal Ripken Sr. in 1957, she knew she would have a baseball life. That year, her new husband was in his first season as a minor-league catcher in the Baltimore Orioles organization. Vi Ripken knew that minor leaguers moved around a lot. But she still wanted to start a family, and so did her husband.

The Ripkens would have four children. Daughter Ellen Leigh was the oldest, followed by Cal Jr., Fred, and Billy. Cal Jr. was born on August 24, 1960, in Havre de Grace, Maryland. And while the family would always call nearby Aberdeen, Maryland, their home base, they moved around constantly while young Cal was growing up.

Cal Sr. did not have a long playing career. While still in the minors in 1961 he hurt his right shoulder and couldn't throw well anymore. That same year, he became a playing manager of the Orioles' Class-D team in Leesburg, Florida. He caught a few games while managing for the next couple of years, then decided to continue in the game strictly as a minor-league manager.

His family followed him from city to city. The Ripkens would live in 14 different towns in 10 different states over an 18-year period. That wasn't always an easy way for kids to grow up, Cal remembers. "My mom was the one who packed up the station wagon," he said. "She held everything together, no doubt about it."

He also remembers how it made him feel to have his father away from home so often. "I didn't like that," he explained. "There are a few times when you're growing up when you need your father. When he wasn't there, it was really traumatic."

Young Cal learned early that one way to spend time with his father was to go out to the ballpark with him. He began doing that whenever possible. "I thought [going to the ballpark with him] was the coolest thing," Cal said. "Looking back on it, the 30 minutes when we drove to and from the park made the whole day."

Cal grew up in a baseball atmosphere. He also learned values from his father that would stay with him forever. Cal Sr. had a tremendous work ethic. To do

As a tall, long-haired youngster, Cal (center) played soccer as well as baseball, and was part of a championship team. That suited him fine because he always liked to win.

a job to the best of his ability, day in and day out, was his way. He also took the old saying "practice makes perfect" one step further. He believed that "*perfect* practice makes perfect." That work ethic rubbed off on his son.

Cal Jr. was also a natural competitor. He played to win from the time he was a youngster. One day, when he was about 6 years old, he was playing checkers with a friend. He set up a five-jump move, and when it worked he was was so happy that he leaped into the air. The only problem was that he banged his head on a concrete windowsill and needed stitches to close the wound.

"I grew up in a family where everything was a competition," Cal said. "Everything you did, it was fun, you did well, you tried hard. If you didn't [try hard], it wasn't fun."

When it came to baseball, Cal Jr. was a natural. The young Ripkens were around the game all the time and were introduced to bats, balls, and gloves at a very early age. Time spent with their dad often meant playing catch, taking ground balls, or practicing their batting strokes. But the Ripken kids played other sports as well, such as football, basketball, and soccer.

Neither Cal Jr. nor his brothers were ever pressured into becoming baseball players. Their father always believed that people should do what makes them happy. The boys were left to decide their futures on their own. But all had their father's work ethic: Whatever they did, they did it right.

GROWING AS A PLAYER

During the summers of 1972, 1973, and 1974, the Ripkens lived in Asheville, North Carolina. Cal Sr. managed the Orioles' minor-league team based there, and it was also there that Cal Jr. really became hooked on baseball. He practiced by himself in the backyard, played games with his brothers, and worked with his dad as often as he could.

The Ripken kids all went to the local stadium, where they worked in the clubhouse or even helped to sell candy in the grandstand. Cal served as the team's batboy for awhile. He also went out to the stadium early with his father, took ground balls, and had a chance to hit.

By the time Cal Jr. began playing Little League he was ready to make his mark. The Asheville team he played for won the state championship one year and went all the way to the southeastern regionals in St. Petersburg, Florida. Cal was a pitcher and infielder and, even then, showed winning form.

In 1975, Cal Sr. was made an Orioles scout and was based in Baltimore. A year later he would become an Orioles coach under legendary manager Earl Weaver. The family could now live in their Aberdeen home all year round. It was just in time, too: 14-year-old Cal Jr. had entered his freshman year at Aberdeen High School in the fall of 1974.

Cal was not big for his age. As a freshman, he weighed just 125 pounds (57 kilograms). He was a pitcher and a shortstop, but got off to a slow start in his high school baseball career. His batting average was under .100 that first year. But, after working with his father during and after the season, he improved his technique at the plate.

In his sophomore and junior seasons, as young Cal grew bigger and stronger, the results showed in his hitting. When he was just 15, his father took him out to Memorial Stadium, the Orioles' ballpark at the time, and held a batting practice with his son. That's when Cal Jr. hit his first home run in a big-league park.

The summer after his junior year of high school he played with the Putty Hill Optimists in the Mickey Mantle League, which was for kids aged 16 and younger. Only the best players were chosen to make the equivalent of an All-Star team, and Cal was picked as

Cal was a pitcher as well as an infielder on his high school baseball team. His strong arm made him an outstanding mound prospect, but his desire to play every day led to his decision to become a full-time infielder.

both a pitcher and shortstop. His overall play with Putty Hill was outstanding, and he was beginning to think, like his father, that he might be able to play professional baseball.

At the same time that his play on the field was improving, he was getting a baseball education of another kind. Many nights, Cal would drive to Memorial

Stadium to pick up his father. In the clubhouse after Orioles games, he would get to talk with many of the players, all of whom already knew him well.

"I was really into baseball by this time," Cal recalled. "Every night when we drove home I asked my father questions about my game and the Orioles' game. I was beginning to understand the game much better and to think like a baseball player."

By the time Cal returned to Aberdeen High for his senior year he was ready. He had always been an Honor Roll student as well as an outstanding athlete. Math was his favorite subject, and he was already thinking about studying that subject if he went to college. But the lure of baseball was too strong.

In the spring, he knew there would be major-league scouts at his high school games. Cal found that very exciting and, as the team's best player, knew they were looking at him. He had grown to 6 feet 2 inches (188 centimeters) by this time and weighed a solid 185 pounds (84 kilograms). He finished the year with a 7–2 record and an excellent 0.79 earned-run-average as a pitcher. But Cal was also becoming a force at the plate. He batted .492 as a senior, with 29 runs batted in during the team's 20-game season. He was also the leading hitter in Harford County.

Aberdeen won the Maryland Class A championship with Cal throwing a two-hitter and striking out 17 in the title game. Cal had finished his high school career on a high note. At the season's end he was voted "Graduate of the Year" by the Amateur Baseball Congress.

But what next? Cal knew now that he wanted to play professional baseball. But would he try it as a pitcher or a shortstop? In pro ball, he couldn't do both. The reasons behind Cal's decision reflected the attitude that would later keep him in the lineup day in and day out.

"Pitching is great when you're out there on the mound," he said. "But what do you do the four other days [if you're a starter]? I wanted to play every day because I liked the action. I wanted to be in the lineup [every day]."

ROOKIE OF THE YEAR

It was no surprise that Cal hoped to be drafted by the Orioles. After all, his father had been in the organization for years and was now a coach. Cal Jr. had grown up around Memorial Stadium and had known many of the Baltimore players. His favorite was Hall of Fame third baseman Brooks Robinson, one of the team's all-time greats.

Cal got his wish when the Orioles made him their third pick in the second round of the draft. That meant that 47 players were chosen before him. Low draft choices like Cal couldn't expect a huge bonus—he signed for $20,000, payable in two equal installments. Cal made sure to plan ahead. His signing agreement with the Orioles included a complete four-year college scholarship. If things didn't work out, he would go to college and get a degree.

Cal was not quite 18 years old when he signed with the Orioles in June 1978. He was sent immediately to the Orioles' Bluefield, West Virginia, team in the all-rookie Appalachian League. Some people in the organization felt that his potential was as a pitcher. But they also liked the way he hit as well as his enthusiasm to play every day. So at Bluefield it was decided that he would play shortstop.

Cal was shaky at first, especially in the field. He had a number of multi-error games before settling down. At the plate, he hit pretty well but showed virtually no power. That was a concern since he was a big, strong kid. Once again, however, he received encouragement and instruction from his father. "Dad assured me that power comes from [a hitter] waiting on the ball," Cal said. "[He said] most young hitters have trouble waiting."

In 63 games for Bluefield, Cal hit .264 with just seven doubles and one triple among his 63 hits. He had only 24 runs batted in and made 32 errors in the field. It wasn't the greatest of debuts. But that winter, Cal played in the Instructional League in Florida and belted two long home runs. The power was coming.

In 1979 he played at Miami in the Florida State Class A League, where he divided his time between shortstop and third base. He batted .303, made the Class-A All-Star team, and led the league in doubles with 28. At that time, Cal considered himself a better third baseman than a shortstop. "At shortstop, I'd been having problems putting it all together," he said. "Playing third, the ball gets to you faster and you just react. I played third base very well from the time I got to Miami."

Over the next two years, Cal improved steadily. At Charlotte (North Carolina) in 1980, Cal discovered his power stroke. He walloped 25 home runs while hitting .276 and driving in 78 runs. The next year, Cal went to his first Orioles spring training camp. He had hopes of making the team, but was sent to Rochester (New York) to play Triple-A ball in 1981.

Some people felt that the Orioles were keeping Cal Jr. around because of his name. But when he slammed three homers in a game against Charleston, he began showing everyone that he was, indeed, major-league material.

By the first week in August, Cal was hitting a solid .288 with 23 homers, 31 doubles, and 76 RBIs in just 114 games. He might have been called up to the Orioles earlier, but there had been a mid-season players' strike in the big leagues that lasted 50 days and interrupted the season. When it resumed, the teams were allowed to add two players to their rosters. On August 8, Cal learned that he was going to the major leagues. He wasn't quite 21 years old.

Cal started the 1981 season with the Rochester Red Wings, a Triple-A minor-league team. He was so good, however, that the Orioles called him up before the year ended.

Cal traveled to Memorial Stadium with his dad that first day. The only advice that Cal Sr. had was for him to "play within yourself." They both knew that Cal's talent and the Ripken work ethic would take care of the rest.

Cal's major-league debut wasn't dramatic or glamorous. He went into a game as a pinch runner. His first hit would come six days later, a single off pitcher Dennis Lamp of the Chicago White Sox. Cal was only a part-timer that year, playing in just 23 games and seeing action at both shortstop and third base. He hit just .128 with five hits in 39 at bats—all singles.

Cal started the 1982 season as the Orioles' third baseman. On opening day against the Kansas City Royals, he hit a two-run homer in his first at bat against righthanded pitcher Dennis Leonard. He circled the bases as if he were on air.

He had two more hits on that day, making it look easy. But baseball is never easy. After that, Cal went into a horrible slump. He got just four hits in his next 55 at bats. It was the kind of thing that could destroy a rookie's confidence. "I couldn't even hit [off] my Dad during batting practice, which I'd been doing since I was a teenager," Cal remembered.

When Cal was switched from third base to shortstop midway through the 1982 season, he had to learn to make all the plays. It wasn't long before he could turn a double-play with the best of them.

Cal's biggest fear now was that the Orioles would give up on him and ship him back to the minors. Manager Earl Weaver tried to reassure him. "[Former third baseman] Doug DeCinces is gone," the manager said. "You're all I've got."

By May 1, Cal was hitting an anemic .117 with just seven hits in 60 at bats. But the next day he got a couple of scratch hits, and after that he began coming out of the slump, hitting well and with power.

On May 29, Cal missed his third game of the year with a minor injury. The next night he returned to the lineup against Toronto. No one knew it then, but that game had historical significance. It marked the beginning of Cal's incredible streak. He would not miss another game for the next 15 years—not a single one.

Cal was playing a very solid third base. From April 24 through June 14, 1982, he went 44 games without committing an error. When he came to the ballpark on July 1 and looked at the starting lineup, he was surprised to see that manager Weaver had moved him over to shortstop. Apparently, it was something the manager had in mind all along.

By that time, Cal was 6 feet 4 inches (193 centimeters) and weighed 210 pounds (95 kilograms). Very few major-league shortstops have been as big. But Weaver felt that Cal could be a very dependable, consistent shortstop. He didn't care if Cal wasn't as quick or acrobatic as some of the smaller shortstops. If a shortstop can make all the routine plays, Weaver reasoned, the team can win with him. "If [the switch] doesn't work," he said, "Cal can always go back to third, where we know he can do the job."

The manager felt that if he had a power-hitting shortstop, and could find another strong hitter to play third, the Orioles would have one up on every other team. Always eager to try, Cal was more than willing to make the change. "It was almost like starting over," he said. "I knew the basics of the position and was very deliberate on the field. [Second baseman] Rich Dauer helped me with positioning. And with each new play that came up and that I handled, my confidence grew. I'd say, 'Okay, that's one more you know you can make.' Pretty soon most of them were taken care of."

Cal remained at shortstop for the rest of the season and when it ended had established himself as a future star. Playing in 160 games, he finished the year with 158 hits in 598 at bats for a .264 average. Considering his terrible slump at the beginning of the season, that was a solid average. He also had 32 doubles, five triples, 28 home runs, and 93 RBIs. All the hard work had paid off. After the season ended, Cal was named American League Rookie of the Year.

Cal surprised a lot of people when he clubbed 28 home runs to help him earn Rookie of the Year honors in 1982. Fans were becoming accustomed to seeing his big power stroke from the right side of the plate.

ON THE WAY TO STARDOM

The 1982 Orioles had been a very solid team, finishing at 94–68, just a single game behind the Milwaukee Brewers in the American League East. Longtime manager Earl Weaver decided to retire that season. Cal hoped his father would be named the new skipper, but Cal Sr. remained the third-base coach and another veteran baseball man, Joe Altobelli, took over the reins.

The Orioles had another good team in 1983. Cal and Eddie Murray would be the top hitters, and they had plenty of support. Cal was hitting third in the order in his second season, ahead of the powerful Murray. Cal didn't slump at the start this time, keeping a steady pace at the plate as the Orioles battled the Detroit Tigers, the New York Yankees, the Toronto Blue Jays, and the Brewers in a tight American League East race.

At mid-season he was selected as an alternate for the All-Star Game. Then a month later, in mid-August, both Cal and the Orioles caught fire. From August 13 to September 25, 1983, Cal had 75 hits in 192 at bats for a .391 average. He also had 14 doubles, 9 homers, 40 runs scored, and 30 runs batted in during that span. As a team, the Orioles were 34–10 and would go on to clinch the American League East title.

When the regular season ended, the Orioles had a 98–64 record, finishing six games ahead of Detroit (92–70) and seven ahead of the Yankees (91–71). A number of the team's players produced fine seasons. Eddie Murray, for example, hit .306 with 33 homers and 111 RBIs and had become one of the American League's top sluggers. But it was the season produced by second-year shortstop Cal Ripken that was the most amazing of all.

Cal had compiled a .318 batting average with 27 home runs and 102 RBIs. But a closer look showed even more than that. He had played every inning of all 162 games. He led the major leagues and set an Orioles record with 211 hits. He

A youthful-looking Cal (right) poses with Dale Murphy of the Atlanta Braves after being named the American League's Most Valuable Player following the 1983 season. Murphy was the National League's MVP.

also led the big leagues in doubles with 47 and was second in extra-base hits with 76. In addition, he was second in the majors in total bases with 343 and led the league in runs scored with 121. Not surprisingly, he was also first in at bats with 663. A look at the records also showed that not one of the shortstops already in the Hall of Fame ever had as many as 211 hits in a season. Cal was just 23 years old. He had come a very long way in a short time.

In the American League Championship Series, the Orioles defeated the Chicago White Sox, 3–1, in a best-of-five. Cal had six hits in 15 at bats for a

.400 average. The Orioles also had great pitching and were now favorites to win the World Series against the Philadelphia Phillies.

The Orioles' pitching prevailed. After the Phillies won the first game 2–1, Baltimore bounced back to win four straight by scores of 4–1, 3–2, 5–4, and 5–0. Pitcher Scott McGregor went the distance in the final game, with Eddie Murray slamming two home runs. The Orioles were world champs. Though Cal was just 3-for-18 in the Series, he had been a major contributor to his team's season-long run to the title.

Shortly after the season ended, Cal was named *The Sporting News* Player of the Year. To top it off, he was also named the American League's Most Valuable Player, winning over teammate Eddie Murray. He looked at the award with a maturity far beyond his 23 years. "Awards are recognition of a job well done," he said. "But *not* winning an award can't take away [your] sense of accomplishment."

THE STREAK BEGINS TO BUILD

By winning the MVP Award in 1983, Cal became the first player ever to capture the Rookie of the Year Award and Most Valuable Player prize in back-to-back seasons. After that, he set about to become the best ballplayer he could be, day after day, year after year. As a team, the Orioles didn't repeat the following season. In fact, during the next five years the team would finish 5th, 4th, 7th, 6th, and 7th. There were no exciting pennant races.

But to Cal, a ball game was a ball game. He gave his best, always played to win, and continued to be one of the top stars in the league. In 1984 he batted .304. A year later, he drove in 110 runs. In 1986 he had 25 homers, making it five straight years that he had hit between 25 and 28 home runs. In 1987 he slumped to .252, but still managed to collect 27 homers and 98 RBIs. These were just some of his numbers. All the while, he continued to play every single game.

In fact, Cal didn't miss a single inning in 904 games. His mark of 8,243 straight innings is believed to be the longest such streak on record. It stretched from June 5, 1982, until September 14, 1987.

During that period, the Orioles made some managerial changes. Earl Weaver came out of retirement to replace Joe Altobelli during the 1985 season. Then, when Weaver retired once again in 1986, Cal Ripken Sr. finally got the job. Now Cal Jr. would be playing for his father.

That wasn't all that happened for the 1987 season. Cal's younger brother, Billy, also joined the team, as a second baseman. He would become the regular second sacker the next season and play for several years alongside Cal. The problem was that the team was pitching-poor, and despite some solid hitting, finished with a 67–95 record in 1987. No one could really blame the manager. As Cal Jr. said, "The 1987 team Dad inherited bore no resemblance to the team that had won the World Series four years earlier."

There was another milestone for Cal following the season. On November 13, he married his longtime sweetheart, Kelly Geer. He and Kelly had met back in 1983. Because Cal had grown up around baseball, he knew how demanding it could be. He saw something in Kelly that made him feel she could handle it.

"I think her independence was the first thing that attracted me to her," Cal said. "She seemed to be doing her own thing and be able to take care of herself and everyone around her." Cal and Kelly went on to have two children. A daughter, Rachel, was born in November 1989, and a son, Ryan, was born in July 1993.

By the 1988 season, the only thing that wasn't going well was the Orioles as a team. Billy Ripken had taken over at second, so the team's double-play combination was Ripken and Ripken. And the manager, of course, was also a Ripken. But when the team lost its first six games of the season, Cal Sr. was fired and replaced by former Orioles superstar Frank Robinson. Cal Sr. returned to being a coach. This wasn't easy for Cal Jr. to swallow. But being a professional, he said little. He later admitted that he felt deeply for his father and knew that the firing must have been painful after 31 years of loyalty to the Orioles organization.

As is often the case, the managerial change didn't make any difference. The team kept losing and wound up with a record 21 straight losses before finally

Things couldn't have been better for the Ripkens in 1987. Cal Sr. (center) had just been named the Orioles' manager, while younger brother, Billy (left), joined the team as a second baseman. Cal Jr., of course, was already an established star at shortstop.

Cal and his wife, Kelly, were married in 1987. They have two children: son Ryan and daughter Rachel. Cal likes nothing better than to spend his free time with his children, and his friends' kids, as well.

winning one game. They would end up losing 107 games. Cal managed a .264 batting average with a career low 23 homers and 81 RBIs. Though the team bounced back somewhat in 1989, Cal had, for him, another average season (.257, 21 homers, 93 RBIs). It was a year later, in 1990, that he really began attracting national attention.

When Cal took the field on June 12 of that year it was a milestone. He was playing in his 1,308th consecutive game, giving him the second-longest consecutive game streak in baseball history. It was a great achievement, but very few people thought he could pass Lou Gehrig for the top spot.

Gehrig was a Hall of Fame first baseman of the New York Yankees and one of the greatest players ever. The "Iron Horse" had a .340 lifetime batting average with 493 career home runs and 1,990 runs batted in for third-best on the all-time list. On top of all his other achievements, Gehrig played in an incredible 2,130 consecutive games.

Gehrig's streak ran from June 1, 1925, to April 30, 1939. It would have lasted even longer had it not been for a cruel stroke of fate. In 1939, Gehrig removed himself from the lineup because his skills seemed to be fading quickly. He soon learned that he had a fatal muscle disease with no known cure. Gehrig died from the disease in 1941, and the illness today is known as Lou Gehrig's Disease. There is still no known cure.

From the day he left the Yankees' lineup in 1939, baseball people felt that Gehrig's streak would never be topped. Now Cal Ripken had played in 1,308 straight. He was still 823 games from breaking Gehrig's mark. In 1990, Cal was 30 years old and in his 10th big-league season. Very few people felt that he could go another 823 games without an illness or an injury—something that would cause him to miss a game.

Some felt that Cal should preserve his health by taking a day off now and then. They thought that by playing every day, Cal might begin to wear down prematurely.

Though he was always willing to put his body on the line, Cal hadn't missed a game since his rookie year. On June 12, 1990, Cal played in his 1,308th straight game, giving him the second-longest playing streak of all time. Through it all, he continued to be one of the game's top stars.

THE BASEBALL WORLD BEGINS WATCHING

Cal hit a career-low .250 in 1990 with 21 homers and 84 RBIs as the Orioles were again a losing team at 76–85. Despite that, he was in the midst of a solid career. The fans had voted him an All-Star starter every year since 1985. Even though he didn't hit that well in 1990, he had set a major-league record for shortstops with a fielding percentage of .996. In addition, his three errors were the fewest for a major-league shortstop in a season. And his 95 straight errorless games that season also set a major-league record, as was his 431 straight chances without a miscue.

Because the Orioles had only contended for a division championship once since 1983, Cal was drawing more and more attention because of his amazing playing streak. People wanted to know more about Cal Ripken Jr. and what drove him to play baseball without rest for so long.

Cal was a big man. He had filled out to a solid 225 pounds (102 kilograms). He seemed to have boundless energy and pushed himself to the limit, even in off-season pickup basketball games. "It can be the last game of the night, and he gets mad when everyone is tired and he's still going," said Orioles pitcher Mike Flanagan. "He's non-stop. Everyone else is gassed, and he's dunking."

Cal connects for a three-run homer off Montreal's Dennis Martinez in the 1991 All-Star Game in Toronto. His round tripper in a 4–2 American League victory earned him MVP honors. He also won the All-Star home-run hitting contest, and when the regular season ended, was named the American League's MVP for the second time.

Cal had always had an innate desire to win, as well. His competitiveness made him want to be the best, no matter what. Orioles outfielder Brady Anderson put it this way: "He doesn't ever want to lose, even in tiny games. He makes up games, like sockball [baseball played with a taped-up sock] in the hallway during rain delays. He's sweating his butt off, then goes out and gets two hits."

Because he had hit a career low .250 in 1990, Cal worked even harder in the off-season. Among other things, he had to deal with self-doubts. "I got away last year from what made me successful," he said early in 1991. "I looked in the mirror and asked, 'Is my talent dwindling?' Instead of thinking that you're going to have a long career, you're doubting yourself, worrying. This year I've gotten things more in focus, and it's taken away any doubts."

If Cal faltered somewhat in 1990, he soared in 1991. The Orioles, however, continued to struggle. The team had just a 13–24 record on May 23 when Johnny Oates replaced Frank Robinson as manager. But despite the team's shortcomings, Cal was once again one of the top players in the big leagues.

By mid-season he was up among the league leaders in nearly every offensive category. Once more the starting shortstop on the All-Star team, he won the annual All-Star home-run hitting contest by belting 12 balls into the seats in 22 swings. Then he hit a three-run homer in a 4–2 American League victory and was named the game's Most Valuable Player.

Toward the end of July, Cal continued to perform in outstanding fashion. He reached another milestone by playing in his 1,500th straight game. He was also leading the American League with a .332 batting average, with 21 homers and 61 RBIs. He had struck out only 26 times and made just five errors in the field.

"Cal has no patience for anyone who plays the game incorrectly," said teammate Mike Flanagan. He said that Cal always had a fear of being unprepared and studied every aspect of the game diligently. He knew the league hitters so well that he was rarely, if ever, out of position at shortstop.

Though the Orioles would wind up with a sorry 67–95 record, Cal's star continued to shine. He finished the year with career bests of 34 home runs and 114 RBIs, as well as a .323 batting average. But that wasn't all. He became just the 10th player in major-league history to hit more than 30 homers and strike out fewer than 50 times (48). He also led the majors with 85 extra-base hits and 368 total bases, as well as 73 multi-hit games.

After the season ended Cal won his first ever Gold Glove for fielding excellence, then was named by *The Sporting News*, the Associated Press, and *Baseball Digest* as their major-league Player of the Year. And shortly afterward, he was named the American League's Most Valuable Player for a second time. It was without a doubt his greatest season.

And perhaps no one appreciated his all-around game more than his new manager, Johnny Oates. "[Cal] doesn't have [Jose] Canseco's swing, or [Shawon] Dunston's throw, or Ozzie Smith's ability to come in on a ball," Oates said. "But the bottom line is, if I'm pitching and I have runners at first and third with one out, the one guy I want the ball hit to is Cal Ripken, because I know the game's over. He's boring to watch for one game. But he's a joy to watch for a season."

QUESTIONS ABOUT THE STREAK

Cal followed his MVP season of 1991 with a season in which he hit just .251, with career lows of 14 homers and 72 RBIs. It was a surprising drop-off, something that happens to athletes for no apparent reason. Cal's work ethic had certainly never changed.

The Orioles, on the other hand, had rebuilt to an 89–73 finish. On his 32nd birthday, Cal signed a new, five-year contract worth more than $30 million. But when he began struggling at the plate once again in 1993, some felt it was time to take a rest; that the streak had become more important than the team. Baseball's all-time hit leader, Pete Rose, on the other hand, felt that the streak was a plus, but only if Cal continued to play at the top of his game. "I think the streak is a good thing for baseball," Rose said, "but it's a better thing if the

Though Cal continued to play all-out baseball every day, some thought it was time for him to take a rest. When he slumped badly in 1992, critics said that Cal's playing streak had become more important to him than the team. Cal insisted that he felt fine and didn't need a rest. His job was to play.

player is productive. If he hits .215, is the streak a good thing? Any pressure he's getting is created by himself because of his low batting average and statistics."

It was true that Cal's batting average had been down for several years, except for his great 1991 season. His agent had even admitted that the streak had become something of a burden. The sudden criticism was bothering Cal. Yet he still tried to be as fan-friendly as he could. As teammate Brady Anderson said, "[Cal] signs more autographs than any superstar I know. He doesn't know how to say no."

Cal was also struggling to put the streak in its proper place within his baseball career. He knew that he was not just a guy who had played more than 1,500 straight games. But he felt that people were starting to forget about his overall talent.

"The one thing that weighs on me is that [the streak] has become my identity," he said. "That's what people see me as—the streak. And I have to deal with that in every series in every city."

Despite the distractions, manager Oates felt that Cal would march on to the record. "If he stays healthy, he'll break [Gehrig's] record," the manager said. "Physically, I don't think he gets tired. Mentally, he gets tired. He gets more fatigued by the extracurricular things than by the playing of the game."

Even when he wasn't hitting well, Cal continued to work hard. He amazed teammates by sometimes running on a treadmill for an hour *after* a game. When the team was home, he would often shoot basketballs in his home gymnasium *before* going to the ballpark. And after some night games, he would lift weights until one in the morning. He was in remarkable physical condition and seemed to have limitless energy.

There was one scare during the 1993 season. On June 6, while playing in his 1,790th straight game, Cal twisted his right knee during a melee between the

Despite the growing pressure of the streak and the hard work to keep in top shape as he got older, Cal remained fan-friendly. He was one of baseball's most popular players and, as teammate Brady Anderson said, "signed more autographs than any superstar I know."

Orioles and the Seattle Mariners. He didn't leave the game, but when he awoke the next day the knee was badly swollen and very painful. Cal told his wife that he didn't think he could play that night. When she asked if he could play just for an inning to keep the streak alive, Cal said he didn't want it that way. "If I can't play, I can live with that," he told her. "If [the streak] ends because of this, I'll be at peace with myself. I can accept it."

After two hours of treatment at the ballpark, Cal took batting practice indoors and had trouble hitting because of the pain. "It was as close as I ever came to not playing," he said later.

But as game time neared, Cal took infield practice and was in the starting lineup. In the game, he reached base three times in four plate appearances and in the ninth inning made a long throw off his right leg to nip a batter and help protect a one-run Oriole lead. He was a gamer, all right.

The Orioles finished the 1993 season with an 85–77 record, tied for third in the American League East. Cal's final batting average was just .257, but he bounced back for a solid power year with 24 homers and 90 RBIs. He also led all American League shortstops in assists for a record-tying seventh time. And, as always, he played in every single game.

In 1994 a question of another kind would arise regarding Cal's pursuit of Lou Gehrig's record. Cal was having a bounce-back year at the plate, and the Orioles were chasing the Yankees for the American League East lead. But when Cal played in his 2,000th straight game on August 1 against the Minnesota Twins, there was a shadow hanging over the game. The major-league owners and the Players' Association were in a contract dispute, and the players were threatening to strike.

The two sides couldn't agree, and the strike began on August 12. When the issues weren't resolved in the next few weeks, the remainder of the season, including the World Series, was canceled for the first time in baseball history. The Orioles and Cal had played just 112 games. The final 50 were off the board.

Cal had batted .315 with 13 homers and 75 RBIs. He was second on the team in batting and RBIs to first baseman Rafael Palmeiro's .319 and 76. It had been a fine year despite the sudden ending.

In 1993, Cal tied another record by leading all American League shortstops in assists for the seventh time. He took great pride in his fielding. His intensity and concentration can be seen here as he fields a routine bouncer. Tough or easy, Cal didn't take any play for granted.

No one was pleased by the strike, though the players felt it was necessary. The question was, when would it end? When the dispute wasn't settled during the off-season, there were rumors that the owners would start the 1995 season with replacement players. If that happened, it might end Cal's streak. But like the other big leaguers, he vowed not to cross the picket lines.

That's when Orioles owner Peter Angelos stepped in. He broke with the other owners by saying that there was no way he would field a replacement team if it jeopardized Cal's streak. Some of the other major leaguers even said that

Cal should be allowed to cross the picket lines just to keep the streak alive. That's the kind of respect his peers had for Cal. Finally, he put a stop to the talk. "[Preserving the streak] is not as big a deal as everyone thinks it is. . . . For me, [the decision] is real easy. If no major-league baseball is being played, I can't be playing."

Fortunately, it never came to that. The 1995 season was delayed, but when it got under way, the regular players were back. And if Cal Ripken once again stayed healthy, he would break Lou Gehrig's record and become baseball's all-time Iron Man on September 6.

THE RECORD FALLS

As usual, Cal followed a very rigid off-season workout schedule. He had always vowed to be better prepared to play than anyone else. The gym and workout facility at his home in Reisterstown, Maryland, gave him everything he needed to stay in prime playing condition.

Cal's everyday workout consisted of hitting for 30 minutes in his batting cage. He also angled his pitching machine to fire one-hop grounders to him. And he rigged a tennis-ball machine to fire a grounder every 11 seconds, first to his backhand, then his gloved hand.

In addition, he would run wind sprints in his spikes so he wouldn't lose the feel of running on grass. It was a complete and often exhausting workout, but he did it without fail.

To many people around baseball it almost seemed as if the 1995 season was a countdown to Cal's breaking the record. The Orioles had a new manager in Phil Regan and as a team did not play as well as the two seasons before. The club spent most of the year trying to maintain a .500 record. As for Cal, he was having a solid season—not one of his best, but at least he was consistent.

During the year he became the all-time Orioles leader in bases on balls and runs scored. He extended his American League record for shortstops with his 13th straight All-Star Game appearance, and had two hits in the game. But all the excitement was building toward September. And when it finally arrived, Cal still had not missed a game. The record was all but his, and the hoopla began.

Reporters continued to ask Cal questions about the streak. The closer he came to the record-breaking game, the more people wrote about the great Yankee Lou Gehrig, whose mark Cal was about to topple. "This isn't about someone trying to erase Lou Gehrig from the record books," Cal said. "It's about somebody who wanted to go out and play baseball every day."

As the big day approached, Cal had trouble sleeping. He worried about what he would say when he spoke to the crowd. There were also people suggesting that, as a tribute to Gehrig, Cal should tie the record, then sit out, so they would be co-holders of the Iron Man mark. This, too, bothered Cal.

He told reporters that sitting out would not only dishonor him, but Lou Gehrig as well. "That would imply that the record was a purpose and not a by-product of my simple desire to go out and play every day, which had been Gehrig's desire, too. Lou Gehrig would not have wanted me to sit out a game as a show of honor. No athlete would."

On September 5, Cal played in his 2,130th game, tying the record. The next night, Camden Yards was packed to the rafters, and the rest of the sporting world was watching as well. This was one of baseball's greatest events in years, and just the thing that was needed to help the game recover from the previous season's players' strike. Cal's children, Rachel and Ryan, threw out the first ball of the game. The stands were filled with celebrities, including President Clinton. And Cal, of course, homered that night against the California Angels to lead the Orioles to a 4–2 victory.

When the game against the Angels on September 6 became official after 4½ innings, Cal had broken Lou Gehrig's record. The game was stopped for a long celebration. Here Cal holds son Ryan while daughter Rachel (in cap) and wife Kelly look on. The fans gave Cal a 22-minute ovation.

When the game became official after 4½ innings (it could no longer be postponed because of rain, for example), the fans stood and cheered for an incredible 22 minutes. His 2,131st straight game was in the record book.

After the game, Cal was honored in a special ceremony. Brady Anderson spoke for Cal's teammates. "Cal, you have inspired many teammates," he said. "You have given the nation uncountable memories. Your pride in and love for the game are at a level few others will ever reach. We warmly congratulate you."

Former Orioles great Brooks Robinson, a Hall of Famer and perhaps the most popular Oriole before Cal, also spoke, and in doing so, passed the torch to Cal. "I played baseball here in Baltimore for over 20 years and they called me Mr. Oriole," Robinson said. "But now, Cal Ripken, you're Mr. Oriole."

Finally, it was Cal's turn to step to the microphone. He had thought long and hard about what he would say. "Tonight I stand here, overwhelmed, as my name is linked with the great and courageous Lou Gehrig," Cal began. "I am truly humbled to have our names spoken in the same breath. Some may think our strongest connection is because we both played many consecutive games. Yet I believe in my heart that our true link is a common motivation: a love of the game of baseball, a passion for your team and a desire to compete on the very highest level. I know that if Lou Gehrig is looking down on tonight's activities, he isn't concerned about someone playing one more consecutive game than he did. Instead, he's viewing tonight as just another example of what is good and right about the great American game. Whether your name is Gehrig or Ripken, or DiMaggio or Robinson, or that of some youngster who picks up his bat or puts on his glove, you are challenged by the game of baseball to do your very best day in and day out. And that's all I've ever tried to do."

When it was over, Cal took a slow lap around the perimeter of Camden Yards, shaking hands and high-fiving as many fans as he could. The cheering crowds pressed close to the rail, trying to get a close-up glimpse and to touch their hero. As one writer put it: "His *assault* on [the record] was surely the least dramatic record run of all time. . . . Yet it turned out to be one of the great feel-good events in sports—ever."

CAL KEEPS ON TICKING

Cal's record run almost obscured everything else about the 1995 season. The Orioles were just 71–73. Cal hit .262 with 17 home runs and 88 RBIs. At season's end, Cal was named "Sportsman of the Year" by both *Sports Illustrated* magazine and *The Sporting News*. He was also the Associated Press and United

Press International "Male Athlete of the Year." And the AP voted his breaking of
Gehrig's record as its "Sports Moment of the Year."

But neither awards, accolades, nor record breaking really changed Cal. In
the off-season, he still worked as hard as anyone. And he spent as much time as
he could with his wife and children. In fact, all kids seemed to like being around

*Cal was 36 years old when the 1996 season ended, but still produced 26 home runs
and 102 runs batted in. Here he slams a double against the Chicago White Sox in
May. And, as usual, he didn't miss a single game.*

Cal. "My three kids know that when they go to Rip's house, they're going there for one reason—to play with Rip," Orioles trainer Richie Bancells said. "They *love* him. But no matter how much fun they had, he had more. The adults were all sitting on the side eating and drinking, and there's Rip in the middle of the pool with eight kids hanging on him."

Remembering how he enjoyed riding in the car with his dad, Cal makes it a point to drive his daughter to school whenever he can. And he'll do the same for his son as soon as Ryan is old enough to go to school.

Cal is also one of the few players in today's game who hasn't thought about using free agency to drive his salary up. In fact, he's never considered leaving the Orioles. And over the years, he and Kelly have become part of the community, using their celebrity status to champion a number of charitable causes.

The Kelly and Cal Ripken Jr. Foundation supports adult and family literacy and youth recreational programs in the Baltimore area. In 1988, Cal established the Baltimore Reads Ripken Learning Center, which serves 300 city adults a year, teaching the fundamentals of reading, writing, math, and computer training, among other things. So far, Kelly and Cal have helped raise more than $1.2 million for their Learning Center. Cal has always felt that his responsibility as a star athlete extends far beyond the playing field.

Back on the field it was business as usual, although in 1996 the new Orioles manager Davey Johnson moved Cal to third base for six games. He played well, but when his replacement at shortstop didn't hit, Cal was returned to his original position. The Orioles had a powerful team that walloped 257 home runs to break the major-league record at the time. They finished at 88–74, second to the Yankees (who would go on to win the World Series), and made the playoffs as the wild-card team.

Cal was 36 years old when the season ended, but once again had a bounce-back year. As always, he played every day, extending his great streak to 2,316

In 1997, Cal was moved from shortstop to third base. It didn't take long for him to adjust. Here he dives to snare a hard grounder off the bat of Boston's Tim Naehring in an April 24 game at Camden Yards.

consecutive games. Better yet, he hit a solid .278 with 26 home runs and 102 runs batted in. It was the fourth 100-RBI season of his career, but his first since 1991.

In the best-of-five division series, the Orioles topped the Indians in four games, with Cal hitting .444 with eight hits in 18 at bats. In the American League Championship Series, a best-of-seven, the Orioles were beaten by the Yankees in five games.

In 1997 the Orioles were even better. They were a solid, all-around team. During the off-season, the team signed Mike Bordick, a slick-fielding short-stop. Now, Cal's move to third base would be permanent. He had, of course, played third base a great deal in the minors. As usual, his attitude was totally professional. "Move me to third and I'll try to be the best third baseman in the league."

Cal played extremely well at third. Though he was 37 in August, he still had the quickness to go to his left and right, and his strong arm enabled him to throw out many runners. With outstanding players at almost every position, strong starters, and an outstanding short relief pitcher in Randy Myers, the Orioles were in first place all season. They finished at 98–64, two games ahead of the rival Yankees.

Once again, Cal played in all 162 games, running his record streak to 2,478 games. Even though a strained back caused a slump in September, Cal batted .270 with 17 homers and 84 RBIs. He was an All-Star once again and played a very strong third base in that game. The one thing he wanted was a second World Series ring to go with the one he helped the Orioles get in 1983.

That, however, wasn't to be. In the division series, the Orioles toppled the Seattle Mariners in four games. But in the American League Championship Series, Cal's team was disappointed again. Though they were the favorites, they were beaten by the Cleveland Indians in six games. It was a tough loss for Cal and his teammates.

Though he hated losing, Cal finished the year on a strong note. He hit .438 in the four games against the Mariners, and followed that with a .348, one-homer performance in the games against the Indians. There was little doubt that he was still a productive ballplayer.

With the streak again the center of attention in 1998, Cal finally decided to end it. On September 20, he voluntarily took himself out of the lineup. Cal's incredible streak ended at 2,632 games. The next day he was back at third, as usual.

In his career, he has set other records in addition to the streak, including the most home runs and most extra base hits by any shortstop in baseball history. But perhaps more than anything else, Cal will be remembered for the way he played the game—his consistency, his work ethic, his loyalty, his preparedness. As his agent, Ron Shapiro, has said, "[Cal] wants to be appreciated for his totality as a human being. . . as a thoughtful, caring, committed, and community human being."

As a ballplayer, Cal still looks forward to playing the game—every day. Some years ago, former teammate Randy Milligan said of Cal, "I've never heard him say 'I'm not feeling so good today.'"

"What I really hate," Cal once said, "is that every time I get in a slump, they said it's because I'm tired from playing so much. . . . It's not fair."

It's not fair because it's not true. Cal has never been tired of playing. It's a work ethic he absorbed from his father, and it has stayed with him all his life. He was hired to do a job and he does it right—every single day.

Cal played extremely well in the 1997 playoffs. Here he belts a long two-run homer against the Cleveland Indians in the American League Championship Series. Unfortunately, the Orioles were beaten in six games.

CAL RIPKEN JR.: HIGHLIGHTS

1960   Born on August 24 in Havre de Grace, Maryland.

1978   Pitches to a 7–2 record and bats .492, leading Aberdeen High School to the
        Maryland Class A championship.
        Selected by the Baltimore Orioles in the second round of the draft.

1982   Named American League Rookie of the Year after hitting 28 home runs and
        driving in 93 runs.

1983   Wins American League Most Valuable Player (MVP) award with a .318 batting
        average, 27 home runs, and 102 RBIs.
        Plays every inning of every game for the Orioles, as the team goes on to win the
        World Series.

1987   Completes a streak of 8,243 consecutive innings.
        Hits at least 25 home runs for the sixth-straight year.
        Joined on the Orioles by younger brother Billy, as Cal Ripken Sr. takes over as
        manager of the team.

1989   In November, daughter Rachel is born.

1990   Plays in his 1,308th-consecutive game.
        Sets several records for shortstops, including a fielding percentage of .996 and 95
        straight errorless games.

1991   Named MVP of the All-Star Game.
        Named American League MVP.

1992   Wins second-consecutive Gold Glove award at shortstop.

1993   In July, son Ryan is born.

1995   Breaks Lou Gehrig's long-standing record of consecutive games played with his
        2,131st game.
        Named "Sportsman of the Year" by numerous magazines and news services.

1997   Elected to the American League All-Star team for the 15th straight year.

1998   Voluntarily ends streak of 2,632 consecutive games played on September 20.

FIND OUT MORE

Adler, David A. *Lou Gehrig: The Luckiest Man Alive*. San Diego: Harcourt, Brace and Co., 1997.

Bjarkman, Peter C., and Warren Spahn. *Earl Weaver*. Broomall, PA: Chelsea House, 1994.

Joseph, Paul. *Cal Ripken, Jr.* Minneapolis: Abdo & Daughters, 1997.

Savage, Jeff. *Cal Ripken, Jr.: Star Shortstop*. Springfield, NJ: Enslow, 1994.

Weber, Bruce. *Baseball Megastars*. New York: Scholastic, 1997.

Web sites:

Cal Ripken Jr.

http://cbs.sportsline.com/u/fans/celebrity/ripken/career/career.html

http://www.sportingnews.com/baseball/players/2035/

How to write to Cal Ripken Jr.:

Cal Ripken Jr.

c/o Baltimore Orioles

Oriole Park at Camden Yards

333 West Camden Street

Baltimore, MD 21201

INDEX